One Tricky Monkey Up on Top

by Jane Belk Moncure
illustrated by Linda Hohag
and Lori Jacobson

Published by

Mankato, Minnesota

The Library —
A Magic Castle

Come to the magic castle
When you are growing tall.
Rows upon rows of Word Windows
Line every single wall.
They reach up high,
As high as the sky,
And you want to open them all.
For every time you open one,
A new adventure has begun.

Melissa opens a Word Window.
Guess what she sees?

A circus train is coming down
the track. Clickety-clack.

"Help," says a little clown.
"My circus animals ran away."

"One tricky monkey went that way."

"I will find him," says Melissa.

Melissa looks for one tricky monkey on the road.

All she finds are hopping toads. How many?

Now Melissa looks in a coconut tree.
What does she see?

"Monkey," she says. "Come with me."

But the monkey is full of tricks. He puts coconuts on his feet.

How many?

Then he stands on his head.

Melissa puts one tricky monkey in Car Number One.

"Who belongs in Car Number Two?" asks Melissa. "Two seals," says the clown.

Melissa looks for two seals in a boat.

All she finds are fish on a line. How many?

Then she looks for them on an ice float.

What does she see?

"Two seals, come with me," says Melissa.

She puts the seals in
Car Number Two.

But what does the tricky monkey do? He
tickles a seal and makes it squeal.

"Who belongs in Car Number Three?"
asks Melissa.

"Three lions," says the clown.
"But I must get the monkey down."
"I will find the lions," says Melissa.

She looks for three lions in a truck.

All she finds are pigs and a duck.
How many?

Then she looks for three lions in a box.

All she finds are shoes and socks.
How many?

Now Melissa looks for lions in a cave in the rocks. What does she see?

"Three lions, come with me," says Melissa.

She puts the lions in Car Number Three.
The tricky monkey swings down from a tree.
He pulls a lion's tail and makes it wail.

"Who belongs in Car Number Four?" asks
Melissa. "Four hippos," says the clown.
"Tricky Monkey, you come down!"

Melissa looks for hippos in a pen.

All she finds are chicks and a hen.
How many?

She looks in a pool. What does she see?

"Four hippos, come with me," says Melissa.

She puts the hippos in Car Number Four.

Guess who sneaks in through the door?
Who tiptoes on a hippo's nose . . .

then swings away on a fire hose?

"Who belongs in Car Number Five?"
"Five elephants," says the clown.
What does Melissa say?

Melissa looks for five elephants in a house.

All she finds are cats and a mouse.
How many?

She looks under a banana tree.

What does she see? What does she say?

"Now we can do a trick," says the clown,

"if that tricky monkey is still around."

Who is up on top?

You can read these words with Melissa.

elephants

lions

hippos

seals

monkey

The Number Train

1 one

2 two

3 three

4 four

5 five